Gracie Finds H[...]

BY JACOB WILLIAMS

ILLUSTRATED BY MARK SANDLIN

VOICE Today, Inc.   Atlanta, Georgia
voicetoday.org

I dedicate this book to my Mom,
Angela Williams, and her organization
VOICE Today, Inc.
My hope is that Gracie Finds Her VOICE
will touch lives and save a child.

Book design and illustration by Mark Sandlin.
Photoshop production by Laura Nalesnik.
Design production by Felicia Kahn.

Printed in the United States of America by Absolute Book Printing.

Foreword

As a prosecutor of child abuse and sex crimes in New York City with over 15 years of experience, I have seen the horrors of child sexual abuse up close. I can tell you first hand the devastation it leaves in its wake. Early on in my career, I discovered that most children do not immediately disclose when they are being sexually abused. As a result, the abuse often continues and escalates. Over the years, I have asked children why they did not tell right away. The answer that comes up repeatedly is simply "He said it was our secret." It occurred to me that children needed to be taught that their bodies are private. They needed to hear that no one has the right to touch their private parts and if someone touches them, to tell a parent or teacher right away. I was inspired to write a children's book called My Body Belongs to Me to teach 3-8 year olds these important lessons.

When it comes to child sexual abuse, secrecy is the most powerful weapon in a predator's arsenal. Children should be encouraged to tell their parents about things that happen to them that make them feel scared, sad or uncomfortable. If children have an open line of communication, they will be more inclined to alert an adult to something nefarious before it becomes a problem. Gracie Finds Her Voice is a simple tale that teaches an important lesson about how keeping secrets can impact a child. In a playful way, children will learn that keeping secrets is not healthy. This book will empower youngsters with the knowledge that no one should put them in a position to have to keep a secret – especially someone they love. It is a great tool to begin a vital discussion that should continue as the child gets older.

I encourage families to institute a "No secrets" rule. The way to effectuate this rule is as follows: If someone, even a grandparent, were to say something to a child such as "I'll get you an ice cream later, but it will be our secret," firmly, but politely say "We don't do secrets in our family." Then turn to the child and say "Right? We don't do secrets. We can tell each other everything." Often families are in search of a word that conveys a similar meaning. I suggest the word surprise as it connotes something that is not being shared right now, but will soon be shared.

Predators know how to get to our youngsters. They know what children want and how to secure their silence. It is time we arm our children with information that can keep them safe. Gracie Finds Her Voice is an important first step in that direction.

Jill Starishevsky
Prosecutor, Child Abuse/Sex Crimes NYC
Author, My Body Belongs to Me

VOICE Today is a non-profit organization whose primary goal is to protect the innocence of children by offering valuable tools for parents to empower their children to learn personal boundaries, personal power and the importance of open and honest communication. This information will enhance the protection of a child's mind, body and spirit. VOICE Today is excited to present the "I FOUND MY VOICE TODAY" program that will offer parents tools through our mascots GRACIE & GRANT, that will include books, dolls, puppets and music to educate children and empower them in a fun and wholesome way. For more information on these and other children's programs and products please visit www.voicetoday.org.

VOICE Today thanks all our faithful donors that made this book possible and especially our Lifesaver Legacy Partners: Sherry and Jason Dewberry, Debbie McClain, Sonya Parham, Pamela and Neil Schmiedeberg.

VOICE Today also thanks Janique Crenshaw and Savannah College Of Art and Design for their initial contribution of the character concept for GRACIE, featured in all the "I Found My VOICE Today" programs.

Little Gracie loved school
every single, little bit.
She loved the playground most of all
and she loved to run around it.

But she hit her toe on a rock
    and fell and scraped her knee.
The teacher made her go inside
    and have the nurse take a see.

A bandage and a lollipop
  had her feeling better fast.
But when she started back outside
  she heard a noise from her class!

She took a peak through the door,
and saw her friend Grant inside!
He took a toy from the teacher's desk,
"Don't do that!" she cried.

Grant turned around quick
and he looked really mad.
He was Gracie's friend, after all,
so it made her really sad.

"Don't tell anyone Gracie,"
Grant said, "or I will get in trouble!
This can be our little secret."
That idea made Gracie's tummy bubble.

They heard the whistle blow,
        the class was on their way!
    "Promise me Gracie!"
"I promise," she heard herself say.

That night Gracie could not eat.
She felt sick, and knew that she should tell.
But she promised that she wouldn't
and knew that Grant would yell!

When she went up to her room
and crawled into her bed,
her mommy came in,
and patted her on the head.

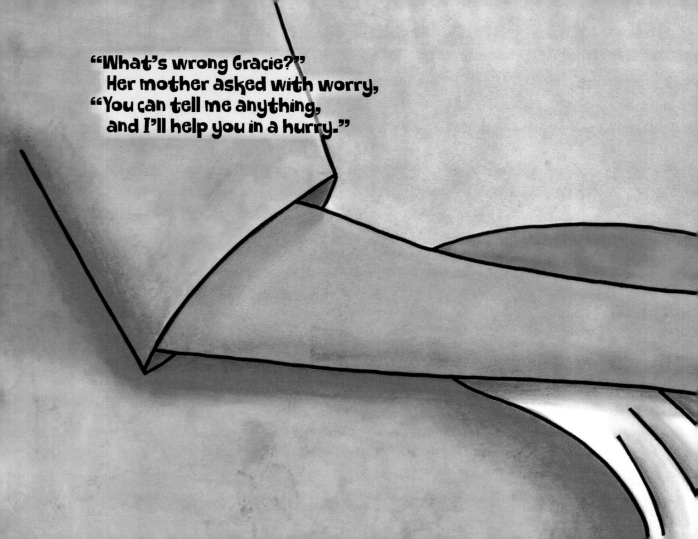

Gracie opened up her mouth
her sweet little head fell.
"I saw a friend do something bad,
but I promised I would not tell."

"Secrets are never good"
her mother said, like she knew.
"They leave you feeling really bad,
and you get stuck in them, like glue."

"So come on Gracie, you can tell me.
When you say it, you will feel better."
But Gracie could not say a word,
no, she could not say a letter.

"Okay Gracie. Maybe later,"
her mother sadly said.
She stood up, turned out the light,
and tucked Gracie into bed.

A fuzzy, purple creature
was sitting on the ground!
And giant colorful flowers
were growing all around!

"This place is awesome!"
said Gracie with a smile.
It was the best she had felt,
in quite a long while.

"I know it is," said the fuzzy thing with a grin. "And you can always come back, if you do something for me again."

His words were really sweet,
and he looked really nice,
but that last little part,
turned Gracie's heart
into ice.

"What do you mean stop speaking?"
she asked with a whimper.
The images around her started to shimmer.

"I do not like that idea,"
Gracie said with fear.
The flowers and colors
all disappeared.

Dark clouds rolled in,
and the light went away.
The magical place,
all turned to grey.

His eyes went dark red,
and his fur turned all black,
he grew nasty claws.
He was a monster,
and that is a fact!

But Gracie stood tall,
no she did not run.
She had been scared all day
but now she was done!

The big furry monster,
took a big monster leap.
And right on top of Gracie,
he fell in a heap.

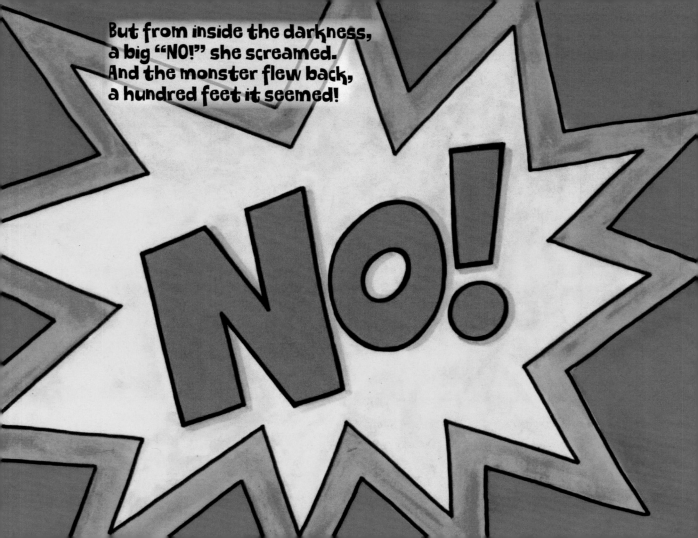

A new Gracie stood up,
all dressed for the fight.
She would never give up her voice,
not when she knew what was right!

Her cape flew out behind her,
a big V glowed on her chest.
She brushed off her hands,
and she handled the rest.

Poof! He was gone,
and the colors all returned!
Gracie could not wait to wake,
and use what she learned!

Her alarm clock went off,
and she shot out of bed,
she went straight to her mom,
and the whole truth she said.

Gracie's mom called the teacher,
who then called up Grant,
who gave back the toy,
then to school they both went.

"It's okay Grant,"
Gracie said with a smile.
"Let me share what I learned!
And let's swing for a while."

Now use what you learned
from Gracie's adventure
to draw your secret you
want to tell.